Traveling with the Underground People

poems by

Vivian Faith Prescott

Finishing Line Press
Georgetown, Kentucky

Traveling with the Underground People

Copyright © 2017 by Vivian Faith Prescott
ISBN 978-1-63534-272-7 First Edition
All rights reserved under International and Pan-American Copyright Conventions.
No part of this book may be reproduced in any manner whatsoever without written permission from the publisher, except in the case of brief quotations embodied in critical articles and reviews.

ACKNOWLEDGMENTS

"Cartography" and "Check the Box" appeared in *Drunken Boat First Peoples* Issue; "Google Sámi" appeared in *Mud City Journal*; "Write Like a Sámi" and "Grandmothers are Cliché" appeared in *Yellow Medicine Review*. Glyph drawings (p. 23 and 10) from Sámi noiade drums; "Archives" collage poem from *Lapponia*, Joannis Schefferi (1800); Collage title "Observant" from Kristian Emil Shreiner, painting by Astri Wellhaven Heiberg (1949).

Publisher: Leah Maines

Editor: Christen Kincaid

Cover Art: Mervi Maarit Salo

Author Photo: Howie Martindale

Cover Design: Elizabeth Maines McCleavy

Printed in the USA on acid-free paper.
Order online: www.finishinglinepress.com
        also available on amazon.com

Author inquiries and mail orders:
Finishing Line Press
P. O. Box 1626
Georgetown, Kentucky 40324
U. S. A.

Contents

Observations of the Lapp Jaw 1

Google Sámi 4

Our skulls are filled with suns... 5

Cartography 6

How to say IT 8

Archives 10

Unleash 11

Noiad 12

Google Search for our Sámi drums 13

Write Like a Sámi 14

All the Sámi Findings.. 15

Grandmothers Are Cliché 17

Check the Box 19

Anthroapology.. 21

Observant 23

Remedy for Assimilation 24

To all my cousins and my community

Observations of the Lapp Jaw

Traveler, trace my face. Lean in. Press your head to mine. Measure me between finger and thumb. I open and close. After we finish, you write something in your notebook. What? I see questions in your eyes. Where do you come from? We've had travelers here before. Some in the daytime, others follow darkness, pursuing the exotic. You say I have protomorphic peculiarities and consider a turned up nose, short stature, projecting cheekbones.

Notes: Four races
1. white
2. yellow
3. black
4. lapplander

A branch of a white-yellow ur-race. Homopaleoarcticus. Homohyperboreus. Hyperbrachycephalic. As the glaciers receded, we developed fine-headed hair. We are local shrunken Paleolithic survivors. In the village, we lined up for measurements and you paused when you saw me. I raised my head slightly. Didn't want to look you in the future. I slipped the two small oranges you gave to me into my coat pocket. Your fingers and figures showed the average female Lapp to have a cranial capacity of 1300.87 cc compared to an average female European capacity of 1300 cc.

More notes:
1. well set limbs
2. black hair
3. broad face
4. stern countenance
5. laziness
6. sorcery
7. temper
8. dirty clothes
9. in possession of drums and stallos

Low stature, tawny (swarthy) complexion, extremely lean, thick heads and prominent foreheads, hollow and blare eyed, short, flat noses, wide mouths, flat faced, meager cheeks, long chin, short, thin, straight, black hair, thin and short beard, strong and active, stooped walk, superstitious, timerous and cowardly: unfit for soldiery.

Years later, in the churchyard, you accompany the priest and two hired hands, digging up a grave. A fine specimen. You put the box in the cart along with the others. And back at the university maybe you sighed—maybe you didn't—when the measurements determined my forehead low and slanting; head squared in form; the lateral projection of my malars.

On the same plane of my malar bones, I swept you forward a few hundred years. And she is in the classroom reading your notes, because the universities of everywhere expected this. Skulls stack the shelves behind her, some with mouths partially open, some with broken and chipped jaws. And more jaws: Jaws with and without skulls, a jaw whose last word still empties forth, a jaw that kissed the space between a newborn's fontanelle, a jaw that sang the moose horns protruding from the riverbank, a jaw that brushed a pubis.

Her stomach is upset whenever she enters this room with you. She is expected to be objective by the objectification. She wants to make paper airplanes with your notes. The professor goes on and on about how apparent it is that Bryn, Czekanowski, and von Eickstedt have only partially accepted the hypothesis of Stratz, Lassila, and Kajava. And there it comes again, the urge to spin around the room, to hover above it. She recalls your annotations, the reason you claim her people are fainthearted is that excessive cold and miserable diet renders their blood destitute of a sufficient quality of spirits. So she raises her hand to her face and notes scarcely any superciliary ridges, taps her narrow nasal entrance.

That night she makes love with her girlfriend on their wet porch. She feels the hard-planked wood beneath her, stares up at the cottonwood leaves falling, her girlfriend's face haloed in the September light. She blinks as the leaves tumble and turn into research notes and then back again. She smells oranges, but she lives on an island in Alaska and the weekly shipment of oranges has missed the barge. Wet leaves stick to her back and slowly her malar fossa forms a slight excavation; and when the alveolar edge of her jaw arches in front, she knows that she knows— due to the natural evolution of her type, brought about during a long seclusion in a changed environment, her chin is rather prominent[1]

---

[1] Her evaluation of the Lapp jaw is still a footnote.

Google Sámi

She is not a myth but a dark imagining. She is a dull murmur in the trees where the wind is praying its sorrowful primal story. But how does this story begin—with either the windswept tundra, or here on this bridge hovering over Sitka's harbor. Beyond, there is no snowpack on the mountains this year. They say the world is melting. She knows how it feels to melt. She walks across the bridge to the coffee shop below. She stirs the black sky in her coffee. Her ancestors once stirred starlight. She opens up her laptop and searches for her anthropological self, her ancestral self, her historical self, her assimilated self. Skridfinn, Saami, Sámi, North Sámi, South Sámi, Mountain Sámi, Sea Sámi. Sometimes she is two seconds away from her people. Or 3,458 miles. Whichever is easier. Whichever fits into this global revolving hypertext markup language spin. Sitka, Alaska to Gáivuotna-Kåfjord, Norway: No Routes Found. Except she is a charged particle like the spirits in the aurora—she uses Google Earth. She is ever-present but appears and disappears, high altitude atomic oxygen colliding, turning red. She wonders how many grandmothers and aunties and cousins you can search for, back-and-forth in time, before the shoe-bands of your world weaken. And below a woman stands alone, chanting in the morning's depthsymmetry, sliding in and out of pitch, tightening her throat, her notes leaping up and down.

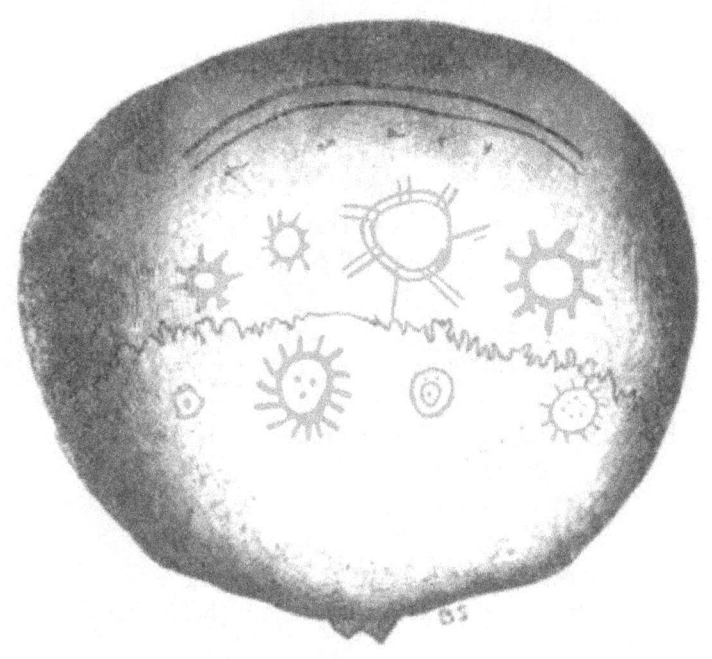

Our skulls are filled with suns

Cartography

Grandmother, you chewed alder
      to red paste,   mixed ash

from woodstoves,   a tincture
      traced on swollen bellies, landmarks

for reindeer traveling   to the sun—
      Charcoal figures: fisher and boat,

hunter's bow,   a conduit   between
      skydome
           and tundra.

You warmed painted hide
      by camplight in the season   before black

robes silenced our   trances.   Now, I peer
      at drummed bellies

beneath a tree rising   from center,
      what remains   hidden

in mountains near *seidda*—rock piles,
      beneath sedge—sun-skins now   mute

behind museum glass. I see your   patterns
      moving   upon *lavvu* walls

sketching tracks to the   pulse   of thumb,
    hooves on the rim of my drum,

        a map

lingering with lichen-scent,   signposts
    herding   my migration toward home.

Seidda: rock piles marking Sámi worship sites. *Lavvu*: Sámi tent. Missionary efforts nearly wiped out our Sámi drums. In the 1600s, Sámi were ordered to dispose of the drums and attend church. Our *Noiade* (shamans) hid themselves and their drums in the mountains. Some families hid drums; others were burned or sold to museums.

How to say IT

say it fast—SÁMI-AMERICAN-AMERICAN-Sámi. Hyphenate.

put some distance between words and generations and peoples

and indigenousness. When they look confused say IT. Grit your teeth but say IT: LAPP, Lappland, lalalalala. SAY IT then SPIT this "IT" out.

runyourwordstogether:indigenousindigenousUS. Not U.S. as in country, but as in peoples. Nod when the young woman says she's a white Indian. Wonder about correcting the corrections and her imperfections and misconceptions. Say Sámi with an "aw." Sigh when she says her mother had her eyes done, unfolded and enfolded the epicanthal fold to blend in with the fold. Her heritage drooping into her line of sight.

Say white-skinned, say light-skinned. Say epicanthal fold and cheekbones. *Epicanthal folds and oblique palpebral fissures* hypotheses— evolutionary adaption to harsh winds and snow, **Blepharoplasty** (Greek: **blepharon**, "eyelid" + **plassein** "to form")

SAY IT. High tone it. Double vowel it. Look IT up on the Internet. Say Sámi with a Sam-i-am. Say IT like a Saami, like a saw, like a cutting blade, like something you had seen. But you are unseen. Hidden. Forbidden. Someone said, "Like a white Indian." Someone said, "I'm 1 % Sámi." Someone said, "You're not from here." Someone said, "You are an alien, a real one from outer space." Someone always said, says, who you are. Define. Classify. Someone said, "You're on the internet." Someone stared at you. Someone said nothing. Someone saw nothing.

Say United Nations Declarations. Guide. Affirm. Concern. Recognize. Welcome. Articles 1 through 46. Theron. Herein. Indigenous. Rights. Right? Yeah, right.

Say it slooooooow. Sámi. Say it with your breath. And when IT comes out of your mouth, know this is the first time. Of many times. Enjoy. Feel IT on your tongue. See IT on your face. Mirror, mirror in the hall on the wall, in books, in the dirty looks, in the anthropological notes. Know you are no Joke. Know this is not the last time you will say IT. Write it. Decolonize it. Hold it. A tight embrace is always a fist. Never let it rest. Carry IT across the ocean.

Sámi.

Archives

Icing too deep, ips
read under the half-moonlamps,

tracing bread crumbs, deep blue taken hold
an ocean of memory - musty snaps...
so warm, here
and other stairs, words jotted here and there,

like footprints wandering over stones and tents
far, not born of this world
now upmarked, but this is ours...

Unleash

We could call up a gale and gust and breeze and storm. We are children of the sun yet rule the wind, a current unwound. We used old songs to claw down trees and pluck gulls from the sky. Our songs were once a secret, handwritten on drum maps, dancing in the half-light of the moon. Now, I use the old songs to soothe bees, to call a soft snowfall, for calling up the wind from a scarlet evening sky, for pleas of sailor and sea. We were once shunned, and yes, hung, and stoned, even burned. The rope in our hands—an ancient method to sing up the wind—untying one knot, then two, then three. For singing. They murdered us. For singing.

Noiade

Stolen by Colonizers: Google Search for Our Sámi Drums

"Their traditional animistic/shamanistic way of life was replaced by Christianity in the 18th century, and today their characteristic drums can only be found in museums." ~United Nations

Write like a Sámi

Be in-di-gen-ous. Write about ancestors, one whose face is weathered, wise and old. Not your old-short-fat-great-grandpa farming fish in ponds in his back yard.

Write like you're a Sámi. Write about drums. Not the imitation drum you ordered online because your sun-cross travels in all directions and you don't know how to heat bend, or how to draw the realm of gods.

Reference the northern lights. Don't write about plate glass and structural steel, but tundra and *lavvu*. Maybe get a Sámi name. Remember how they colonized you, took away your name, and gave you another one. Find a Bath Mother willing to wash it away with boiled alder bark. Call yourself something exotic— the page will take notice of *Ráijá* or *Biehtár*.

Your prose or poem must mention reindeer, or perhaps a noiade traveling with the underground people; their feet against ours, pressing up toward the surface of this world.

Make sure you reveal and divulge and disclose you're a Sámi or they'll think you're new-agey. Call up the spirits when you do: Good spirits, bad spirits, drunk spirits and good-bad-drunks—relatives who floated face down, tangled in a fishing boat's rigging,

cousins who tumbled and rolled in pickup trucks from the highway to the beach below. Mention the spirits peering up from a birch wood cup—the readers and the double-checkers will anticipate this with their hands rubbed together and their head nods, and an ah-ha rigid against their palates.

Mention yoiks.

Write like a Sámi. Refer to raising the wind and smearing butter on your doorframe and tin thread dragged through a die with your teeth. But leave out Y chromosomal polymorphisms and translucency of the iris— you know where that'll lead.

All the Sámi Findings

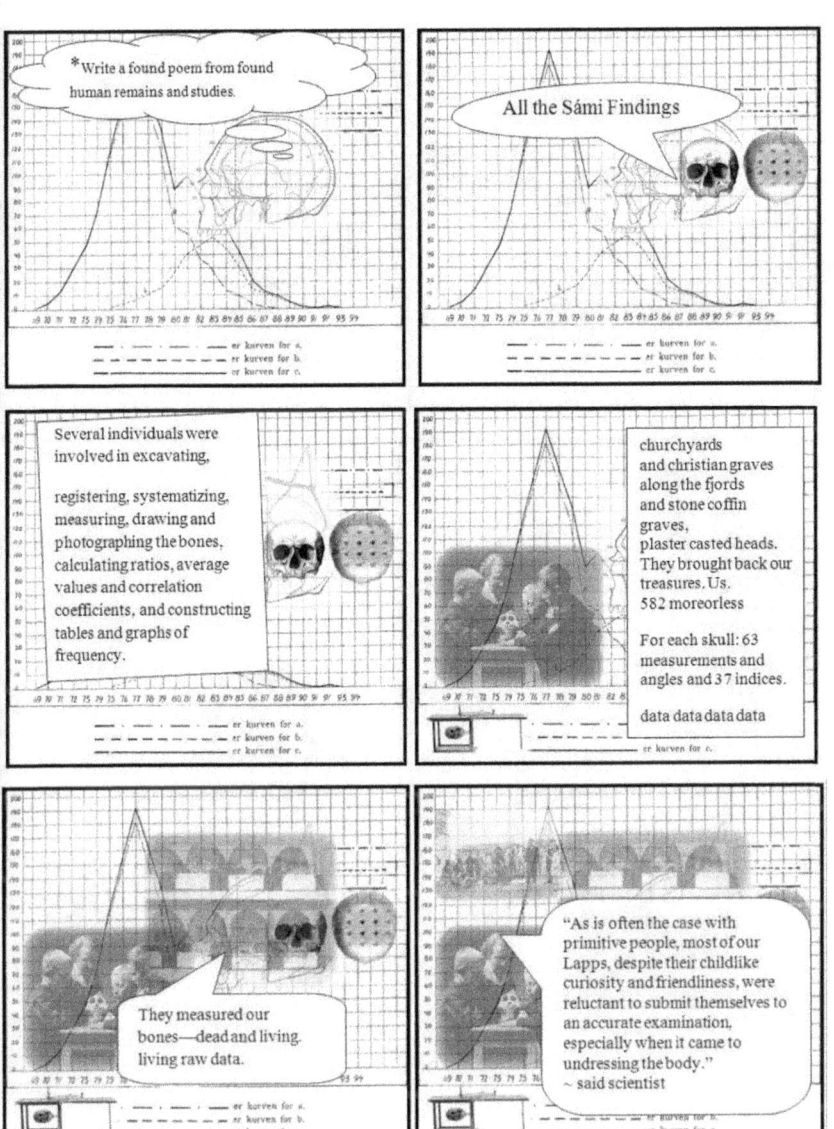

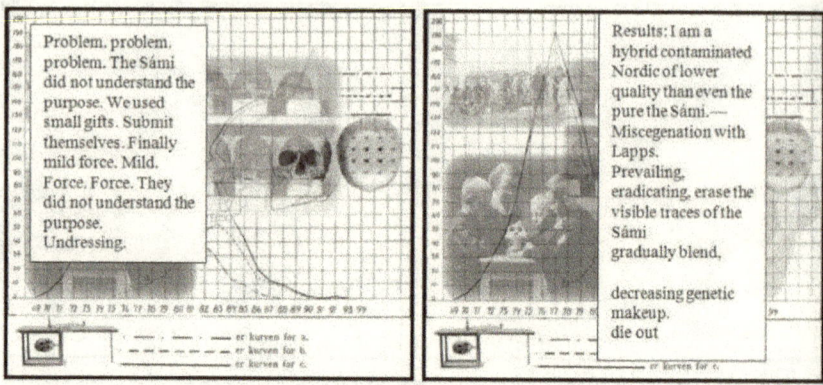
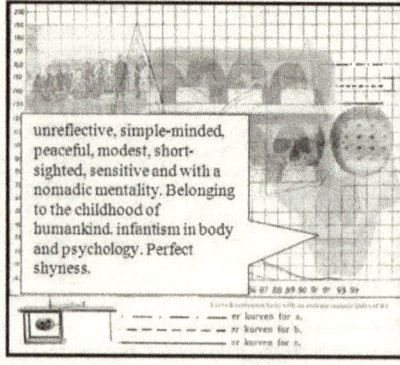
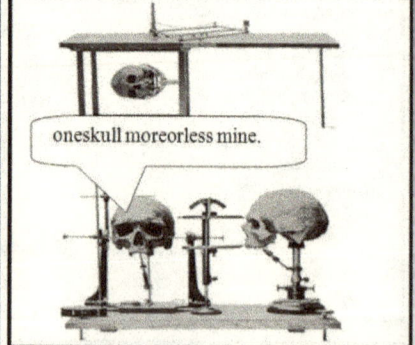

Grandmothers are Cliché
said a writing mentor

Grandmothers crochet and take in four grandchildren and give their daughters breathalyzers before they can see their kids. Grandmothers write copy for Amazon. Grandmothers have Phds and MFAs and take care of their PTSD soldier husbands who return from Iraq kicking and screaming at them, pulling the covers to hide in the dark. Grandmothers' houses are robbed by their meth-head grandsons. Grandmothers sift through the garbage dump on the beach for tossed away metal and glass to make art. Grandmothers weave dance robes. Grandmothers are CEOs signing million dollar language revitalization checks. Grandmothers carve dance masks from alder. Grandmothers harvest fireweed and mountain goat hair and pull cedar bark from trees. Grandmothers blow deer calls made of leaves. Grandmothers play with Ouija boards. Grandmothers fish for salmon. Grandmothers hunt moose. Grandmothers teach 2nd grade. Grandmothers gut deer. Grandmothers lie on the muskeg on their bellies, picking cranberries. Grandmothers fall in love with the young men who work around their houses for the summer. Grandmothers chop wood. Grandmothers practice tsunami evacuations. Grandmothers fall in love with women who sculpt owls. Grandmothers. Grandmothers wipe blueberry stained fingers and blood from their hands—periods flowing and ending, salmon hearts pulsing in their palms. Grandmothers clutch their empty bellies. Grandmothers fill them up. Grandmothers trace scars across their chests and comets across the sky. Grandmothers hold Grandfathers or Grandmothers in the bluedark night. The bluedark night holds Grandmothers. Grandmothers carry grandchildren to medivac planes. Grandmothers feed great-grandfathers, feed grandkids and great grandkids. Grandmothers join wet-t-shirt contests, wash the faces of their brain-dead sons, and slice open halibut. Grandmothers change flat tires on Honda Fits. Grandmothers love the scent of outboard exhaust. Grandmothers offer salmon casseroles at the thresholds of the newly deceased. Grandmothers remember names and then forget names. Grandmothers read Mad Magazine. Grandmothers stand in the dark with one another listening for the humpbacks' song.

Grandmothers love their beer. Grandmothers collect Japanese dolls. Grandmothers march through town carrying signs to save rivers, stop dams and mining. Grandmothers wear hoodies. Grandmothers wear brown rubber boots. Grandmothers smoke cigarettes next to grandkids while eating Mystic Mint cookies and watching Fox News. Grandmothers pick the tails off thousands and thousands of shrimp. Grandmothers sigh when herons fly close to their heads. On the beach, Grandmothers trip on slick wet rocks and fold themselves into holy rites, slicing their cheeks on igneous—Grandmothers lie there waiting in the tidal interval for the duration of rise and the duration of fall.

Check the Box

√ OTHER

Check only One: African American ☐   American Indian ☐
Alaskan Native ☐   Pacific Islander ☐
Asian American ☐   Hispanic/Latino ☐
White/Off white/blue-eyed, brown-eyed/epicanthal fold,
no epicanthal fold ☐

Other: YES ☐   NO ☐

Are you a First Homo-Sapien Inhabitant of Europe?
YES ☐   NO ☐
Are you a Second Generation Homo-Sapien Inhabitant of your American home town?
YES ☐   NO ☐
If yes: 1st, 2nd, 3rd, 4th, 5th generation ☐

How long have you been separated from your people?
10,000 years ☐   5,000 years ☐   three generations ☐
one year ☐   since dinner ☐
Which traditional garments do you wear?
reindeer moccasins ☐
four-winds hat ☐
gákti ☐
Carhartts ☐
feathered headdress ☐

Do you know how to ski? YES ☐   NO ☐

Can you ride a horse? YES ☐ NO ☐

Can you steal a horse? YES ☐ NO ☐

Have you ever butchered a reindeer? YES ☐ NO ☐
    Explain:

Have you ever ridden a reindeer? YES ☐ NO ☐

Do you play the drum? YES ☐ NO ☐

Do you sing weird songs without words in the woods?
YES ☐ NO ☐   I resist the urge ☐

Does your blood contain mtDNA subhaplogroup U5b?
YES ☐ NO ☐

Or mtDNA haplogroup V? YES ☐ NO ☐

Do you identify yourself as something old and discarded, a scrap of clothing? YES ☐ NO ☐

Have you ever heard of a Noaide? YES ☐ NO ☐

Can you call a whale to shore? YES ☐ NO ☐

Do you really think you came from the Sun? YES ☐ NO ☐

Anthroapology

sorry, sorry, sorry.

They said. unlawful intervention. and human rights. right?
But necessary work. well preserved. unique possibilities.
They will keep our bones safe. Safe. wellLit. Secure.
preserved. thank you, Giitu. kind find. Refind that you are.
They measured, pulled the DNA from flesh and bone and stone
and the molecules that carried us spilled out
Results, fragments, instructions in our cells:
                                    Take no notice of wind
                           or sun, but reindeer hooves weaving
                                a path between valleys.
                                        Follow it
                                 until you discover
                                   the fire is cold
                           and only a ring of stones remain.

    Tracks are dreams pressed into spines— walked up our
    backs and down our legs, our long strands spiraling.
    We have been a wolf. hereditary material.

This world is well fed: fish migrate
to deep water, bears gorge on berries,
marmots fill holes with pinenuts
and currants, reindeer eat mushrooms.

    The Wind is the rungs cutting our skin shallower
    here. I sense sharpness beneath my skin: a memory bent
    into rockshapes.

                                We wade the sea. salt salt salt.
                        Brine in your food and in our bodies.
                Our bodies are pale suns. Time perches on the bow
              of our skiffs and our paddle strokes slice the sea.
                                            And us.

We are so long that we can't fit into our own cells. We are
tightly coiled. 23 pairs of hollow hairs. You study my
bones and discover layers of fur, a woolly undercoat.
Our bones breathe cold air, and cool the arteries around
our hearts.

How we inhabit the world: Our lives are nets full of birds
I unfold light, return winter
and ourselves.
Tufts of reindeer hair press into mud.

      This place is a constant hum. Maybe you can see that
      I am backlit, that I am still breathing last night's dream

                and all I can do is borrow a lamp
                  for the long journey back home.
                  It has been a long journey, indeed.

      DNA Material returned. Us. Historical value= 9,000
      years. We divide and copy ourselves, and transform. We
      are newborn calves walking in spring snow.

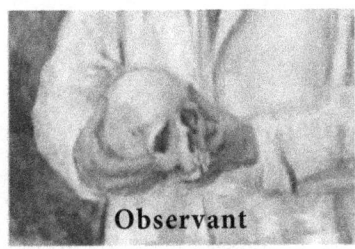

Observant

Tell us how your sight has more teeth than ours, that your gold streets and deliverance give us more hope.

Our antlered heads are our histories— blood-filled and velvet covered. There is no way to separate ourselves

from the deer, or the snow dusting brittle ice. They link and interlink. How can I tell you that this river between realms is not just a myth,

but a story holding me in all worlds.

The story is hung beside the tent in a stretched hide. I keep it padded with moss because it is our fragility.

I keep this story from breaking open. I can disrobe it like skin and like a sun-bleached rag; I hang it in the trees.

Some days I hang it low in the branches or toss it up into the alpine meadow. Some days I lift it high over my head, a ceremony to the sky. No one knows what is inside the skin.

I don't tell. They only guess—they tease me: a tuft of reindeer hair, two silver salmon scales, the north wind, a pinch of coffee grounds, and perhaps a pencil.

Yes, I say, all of those are my hallowed lives.

Remedy for Assimilation

Press a bear's tooth or reindeer jawbone
>on the affected area of the tooth. Learn

to pull poems from your bones.
>Massage your head and neck and tug hair

at the apex of your head, and wash
>your head in hot coffee to heal a headache.

Inhabit the memory of last ice age.
>Have a bag ready to bury with yourself:

It should contain a blue ink pen, dry shoe-hay,
>a round smooth stone, a small notebook.

Leave an offering of reindeer carcasses,
>fish fat and other precious objects at sacred sites

for good luck. Rub corn snow on frostbite.
>Recite an incantation while rubbing a frog

on infected skin. Re-center and re-enter
>identity in this stretch of the river. Recreate

your story to be told to outsiders. Recognize
>collective memory—see your face

carved in a tree. Hang meat in its branches,
>smear it with grease.

Vivian Faith Prescott is a fifth generation Alaskan, born and raised in a multi-cultural family on the small island of Wrangell in Southeastern Alaska. She lives in Wrangell near the Red Alder Head Village site at her family's fishcamp, Mickey's Fishcamp. She holds an MFA from the University of Alaska and a Ph.D. in Cross Cultural Studies. Her poetry has appeared in *The North American Review, Yellow Medicine Review, Prairie Schooner* and *Ghost Fishing: An Eco-Justice Anthology* (University of Georgia Press). Vivian married into a Tlingit family and has four grown children and she was adopted into their clan, the T'akdeintaan, Snail House, and given the Tlingit name *Yéilk' Tlaa*, Mother-of-Cute-Little-Raven. Vivian is the founding member of Blue Canoe Writers in Sitka and Flying Island Writers and Artists in Wrangell with an emphasis on mentoring Indigenous writers. She's a two-time Pushcart Prize nominee and received the Jason Wenger Award for Literary Excellence, in addition to a Rasmuson Fellowship (2015). She's a two-time semi-finalist for the Joy Harjo Poetry Award and a semi-finalist for the Colorado Prize for Poetry. She is the author of two poetry chapbooks, *Slick* (White Knuckle Press) and *Sludge* (Flutter Press), plus a full length collection, *The Hide of My Tongue*, and one short story collection, *The Dead Go to Seattle* (Boreal Books/Red Hen Press, 2017).